Praise for Authors
Jennifer Brozost, M.A. & Vimmi Shroff, M.A.
and their company, PEAS
(Private Education Advisory Service)

Parent Guide News

"Private Education Advisory Service (PEAS) puts parents in the know when it comes to getting children into Manhattan's top schools. PEAS was launched by Jennifer Brozost and Vimmi Shroff, two former private school admissions professionals, armed with more than 15 years of experience dealing with private schools in the City. The duo guides families through the admissions process, from filling out applications, to ultimately identifying the right school for each child. In its first year of business, PEAS helped place 100% of its Pre-K and kindergarten students for the 2010-2011 school year. Visit www.nypeas.com to begin your family's personal success story."

New York Family Magazine

"Navigating in the City's private school admissions process can be a daunting task, a fact which Jennifer Brozost and Vimmi Shroff know firsthand. The two New York City moms boast 15 years of admissions experience at the city's top private schools—and have also gone through the application process themselves with their own kids. Now they've created PEAS, a private education advisory service that helps guide other families through the whole process, from filling out applications to ultimately identifying the right school for your child. Their experience and affordability should make them an appealing choice."

"Jennifer and Vimmi at PEAS made the stressful and terryfying application process into an organized, efficient and almost pleasant experience with fruitful results. Our family felt that we had true partners in our journey for admissions and can't say enough good things about PEAS. Simply outstanding and the best!"—**RS**

Jennifer and Vimmi made the daunting task of kindergarten admissions almost enjoyable. They held our hands and we navigated through the process with intrepid honesty, acute skill and a plethora of class. We were accepted at all three of our top choices—a feat I previously believvfed to be unattainable. Our most difficult decision became which to attend! Believe in miracles with the help of PEAS."—**NB**

"Jennifer and Vimmi are very knowledgeable about each private school. When beginning the process, they helped us select which school would be best for our family. They continued to guide us through with confidence, always making us feel like a priority. Their friendly and calm disposition made it easy for us to contact them with any questions we had. We always received prompt and insightful answers and advice. With their help we were very successful in gaining enterance into our top two choices. They were with us every step of the way. PEAS takes away the stress in a very competitive environment. We thank you for all your hard work."—**SS&CS**

Jennifer Brozost, M.A.   Vimmi Shroff, M.A.

The New York City Private School Admissions Handbook

An Insiders' Guide to the Admissions Process
From Nursery Through On-Going Schools

VIRGO
ebooks

Published by
Virgo eBooks Publishing
New York—Vermont
www.VirgoeBooks.com
office@virgoebooks.com

May 2015

Formatting: Constantin Dancu and Raul Folea
Cover design: Marius Epure

ISBN 13: 978-0692442531

Dedication

We want to thank our wonderful families for constantly making us laugh, learn and keeping us inspired each day.

Contents

Jennifer Brozost, M.A.   Vimmi Shroff, M.A.

The New York City Private School Admissions Handbook

• • • • • • ● ● ● ⬤ ● ● ● ● ● • • • •

An Insiders' Guide to the Admissions Process
From Nursery Through On-Going Schools

Acknowledgments

We are indebted to Lila Suna for her critical reading and editing of our manuscript. Her insights and counsel were invaluable to our writing process, as were her support and encouragement.

We would also like to thank our many clients and friends for their encouragement and for sharing their very personal stories.

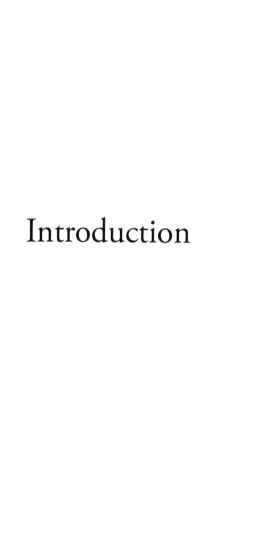

Introduction

We decided to write this book because we wanted to have an easy to understand, extremely user friendly and easy-to-carry guide for families going through the arduous process of applying to New York City private schools for their children.

When we went through the process with our own children, we were both craving an authoritative guidebook that we could put in our purses, refer to before each school visit or meeting and even take notes in as we toured. Instead, we found ourselves juggling file folders packed with Xeroxes of school information, scrambling for paper to jot down our thoughts about each school, or something important we noticed during the tour.

We remember those days. We have come up with such a reference book that gives readers real advice from two experienced women who have worked in the admissions departments of New York City private schools for over 15 years, and that takes you through this uniquely New York crazy process, step by step. It also has pages designed for readers to conveniently record their thoughts and feelings about each school.

We have both been through this process with our own children and years ago we even made some mistakes (yikes) of our own - mistakes that we have learned from. And now, after over 15 years in this business, we are here so that you will have your own personal admissions "experts" to make sure that you do not make any avoidable mistakes.

As you read this book, you will notice that sometimes Jennifer is speaking and sharing her experiences, and other times Vimmi is sharing hers. That is why we go back and forth between using, "We," and using our names.

There are also many personal stories from friends, clients, and anyone who would share relevant experiences with us. These amusing stories appear after each chapter, and are 100 percent true. They are there to entertain, educate and make educate memorable points to you, parents.

Enjoy!

1

Why Am I Listening To These Two Women?

Who We Are

We came from two very different worlds, different sensibilities, and different cultures. Yet we share many common goals, and aspirations.

Jennifer grew up in Philadelphia. She has a Master's in Education from Columbia University with an advanced degree in the Teaching of Reading and Writing. She lives in Manhattan with her husband, Marshall, two children Ari and Sofia and Calvin, their Havanese.

Vimmi grew up in India. She moved to the United States after getting married. She has a Master's Degree in Education from New York University. She lives in Manhattan with her husband, Sanjay, and two boys Vivaan and Sumair.

We have both worked in the admissions departments of the top New York City private schools for over 15 years. We have worked at more than 10 different private schools throughout the city.

We have also navigated this process, successfully, for our own children. Both of us have worked as either directors of admissions and/or admission officers and have been involved in all aspects of the process including interviewing parents, overseeing playgroup visits, and reading thousands of completed files and much more.

What Inspired Us To Write This?

We want to help parents on their journey through the admissions process, with the goal of helping you to obtain one of the 'precious few' acceptance letters.

We have witnessed the innocent mistakes of overwhelmed parents: thank you letters sent or addressed to the wrong directors, parents writing about their educational philosophies that are polar opposite to the school's philosophy to which they are applying, a ten page thesis on a four year old's strengths, couples disagreeing and arguing in the interview, parents' failure to turn off their smartphones, asking too many questions during the group tour, acting completely disinterested, calling the admissions office incessantly or not paying proper attention to the appropriate protocol when applying to schools... to name but a few of the common errors!

We are determined to ensure that parents who read this book DO NOT MAKE THE SAME MISTAKES.

Since we have gone through this labor-intensive and frustrating process with our own children, we have experienced first-hand the challenges of scheduling all the playgroups, meetings, tours and interviews. We have pleaded with our husbands to turn off their Smartphones and smile as we burned through dozens of hours planning and visiting ten different schools. We have tabled disagreements with our spouses until after the parent interviews, and we have fallen in love with schools that were not the right fit for our children (knowing, from our many years of experience, that they would never end up in these schools).

We have been there and we have gotten through it all smiling.

We want to help bright and talented parents who are put in an impossible situation: navigating the crazy and competitive world of New York City private school admissions.

We offer you huge amounts of warmth, caring, and most importantly, expert knowledge that has been accumulated over the past 15 years.

You are getting real advice from our real experiences!

Use this book as your guide for valuable wisdom.

Maintain your sense of humor and keep your spirits up! Look at this as an opportunity to discover many magical and unique schools. We are here to help you navigate through this entire challenge.

Going through this process is so much more than a cerebral one. It is an emotional, crucial, soul-searching time in your life.

In our 15 years of experience we have never found a book that takes readers through this journey with warmth, humor, and most importantly, by offering what only professionals who have worked in admissions can provide: the hard facts on getting in!

This book is a compilation of the experiences, opinions, concerns, complaints, frustrations and remedies that we, and other families, have experienced in the unique New York City private school admissions process.

Sharing our knowledge with you is a true labor of love. Sit down, relax and proceed to the next chapter … We are here to take this journey with you!

Most sophisticated New York parents are prepared for anything that might occur during the process of applying one's child to the many fine private schools in Manhattan... that is, we think we are.

But my experience following a school tour might be unique. We gathered for the Q&A and while the Director of Admissions responded to our questions, one mom began to nurse her baby. The room went quiet for a moment with only one sound –that of the baby's sucking her mother's milk.

While there may be nothing wrong with this behavior in many people's minds, it would probably be a better idea not to do anything that may be perceived as "controversial" or out of the ordinary while visiting schools you may be applying to.

2

It's only March … Should I be Doing Something Right Now?

Admissions season is around the corner. Here are some easy steps to ensure a smooth and painless ride for your family through the frenzy.

Get Organized

One of the most important things you can do now is to get organized! In September you will have so much to do, for both the admissions process and in helping your children become acclimated to their current schools and classes. We know it is overwhelming.

Let's prepare now... you will be a better parent and a better spouse. Trust us, we lived through this. I think my husband has just about recovered from our first bout with trying to get our own son into the right school. I can only imagine what it would be like to go into this process blind as most people do.

Immediately after Labor Day you will need to schedule and attend tours and open houses. You will also need to complete your applications, and attend various playgroups/interviews.

It is truly a full-time job. Treat it as such if you want to maximize your chances for success.

Set Up Your Organizational Tools Now

Buy a calendar or create an Excel Spreadsheet. List all the schools you like with their contact information:

- Phone number
- E-mail
- Mailing address
- Name of Director of Admissions

Each school has its own application deadline. Note all deadlines, open houses, tours and interview dates. It is a challenge to keep track of this, so maintain a folder or calendar that is easily accessible. This will keep you organized and sane. We suggest a duplicate calendar for your spouse.

Invest in a filing system. All correspondence from each school should be saved in date order in their designated folder.

Keep a notebook handy to record your thoughts, impressions and observations of each school. Record your impressions immediately after each school visit so that they are fresh and accurate. (See page 188) This "personal diary" is an invaluable tool to have as you get closer to the decision making process.

Work on your Application Essays Early

One of the most time-consuming and stressful parts of the application process is writing the dreaded essays needed to complete each application. Most essays will ask that you describe your child and will require that you explain why you are applying to their school.

Jot down your child's strengths and weakness. Keep the latter list short!

Once you have chosen four or five attributes, note a brief anecdote that would complement those attributes. This list will ensure that the writing process is easier and more organized. Be realistic and SUCCINCT when describing your child. Remember, admissions staff read hundreds of essays. The more personal and specific the information is, the more memorable your application will be.

Think about your own philosophy or view of education. How does your philosophy match the school to which you are applying?

One of the goals of this process is to gain admission to a school that is the right fit for your family... not just any school that accepts your child!

Application essays will be discussed in depth in Chapter Ten.

Look at Schools with an Open Mind

Opinions, opinions! Everyone has them and when it comes to schools, boy do they like to share them. Unfortunately, there is a lot of misinformation, gossip, and "frenemies" out there.

Frenemies—the type of "friend" whose words or actions bring you down (whether you realize it as intentional or not.)

Frenemies have been introduced to the NYC private school admissions world for parents who have unfortunately faced the grim reality of friends turning foes. We have seen families ostracized from social events, others misled about school choices, trusts broken, back stabbing etc.

Believe it or not, people are competitive and do not always have your best interests in mind, especially when their own children may be applying to the same schools you have selected for your kids.

One of the most productive things you can do now and through this entire process is to completely tune out these opinions. Instead, stay connected with dear friends who already have their own children in the schools to which you are applying. You are not potential competition for their kid's place in the school. Ask them questions and look for their opinions. They will know the "real deal" about the school. They are now experienced members of the school community. They also know you and your child.

These friends will be able to offer sincere insight into whether certain schools are a fit for your family or child. They might even be able to put in a good word with the admissions staff.

It is productive to have well-liked families, already in the school, stop by the admissions office to speak on your family's behalf. Ideally, one parent should pop in to the office during the day to briefly put in a good word if they feel your family would be an asset to the school community. If "stopping by" the office is not a convenient option, then have them write a letter. Keep the letter short and have it state why your family would be an asset to the existing community. This letter of support will be put in your file for all the admissions staff to see when it is time to make final admissions decisions.

Don't Be Too Picky For the Wrong Reasons

Do not rule out schools that are not considered "top tier." In this competitive environment there are few safety schools. The "top tier" designation can be somewhat inaccurate as so many independent schools do a superb job in educating our children. Keep an open mind.

It is critical to seek a good match for your child and family, as opposed to a school that will help you climb the social ladder, give you bragging rights, or make you feel cool among your peers.

If the school is not the right fit for your family or child, all the above will be short-lived because you will be back in this process reapplying to schools that are actually a real match. We see this all the time and we don't want it to happen to you!

Do Your Homework

If all goes well the first time around, this admissions process will be a one-time event. Do your homework, both for the schools to which you are applying, as well as for the entire process.

Learn as much about each school as possible.

By now you have attended some of the spring tours. Open Houses in the fall are another venue for learning more about a school. This is a good jump-start to gain access to schools, meet with their admissions staff, and obtain a "feel" for the similarities and differences among schools. It also allows you to make a positive first impression with key decision makers, which can help you down the road.

Remember the wise saying: "You never get a second chance to make a good first impression!"

School websites are a great resource. Learn as much as you can about their mission statement, history, educational philosophy and physical space. Take the time to read over the school's mission statement. These statements are meaningful to schools that work hard to exemplify the values upon which the school was founded.

What resonates most with you about the school? The more you know about an institution, the more confidence you'll have, and the easier the next six months will be.

My wife and I were feeling like pros by our third spring tour. We knew the drill: show up on time, turn off your cell phone, and showcase what a loving couple we are by exhibiting minor PDA - hand-holding and shoulder squeezes.

We had heard that some schools watch you approach the building via their security cameras so we made sure that any disagreements were done safely inside the cab.

When we began tour three, we thought that we'd be the couple laughing at some well-meaning, but clearly not-ready-for-prime time parents who were guilty of a glaring rookie mistake. Looking back, I see now that it was hubris, pure and simple, that did us in. Hubris and the loudest Velcro in the world.

I had just purchased a hip, expensive messenger bag. My wife determined whether it was an appropriate accessory for whatever school we visited. School Number Three was deemed downtown enough for me to bring the bag. As I looked around I noticed that no other parents had a bag like mine. This could be a good thing or a bad thing. My wife was having the same anxious thoughts. When you become a pro at school tours, you become conscious of how the little things can come back to bite you. Hopefully, I wouldn't be remembered as the "bag guy."

What took our minds off whether the admissions director was drawing a smiley or sad face next to our names was a ludicrously loud, Velcro-tearing sound coming from the direction of my bag. Think of a 747 taking off.

The admissions director paused in her speech. Everyone turned toward me. I think I even saw a surveillance camera rotate toward me... my wife looked away.

I now carry what I need in my pockets.

3

Is Your Relationship with Your Nursery School Director Just as Important as the One with your In-laws?

It is critical to establish a good rapport with your nursery school director. One of the most important aspects of applying to an on-going school is your (good) relationship with your director!

The director serves as the liaison between you and the schools to which you are applying. This association is just as important as the complicated relationship with your in-laws. Sometimes you just have to grin and bear it!

Lay the groundwork for a good pre-school and a successful ex-missions process from the start of your child's first pre-school year.

Increased demand for great schools means more competition. More competition creates a great burden for the director who has the most challenging job of placing every child that graduates from his or her pre-school program into a school of the parents' choice.

Do you want that coveted spot? Then forge an amicable, controversy-free relationship with your nursery school director!

Why is a Good Relationship so Critical?

The key person you will work with throughout the application process is your nursery school director. Although he or she remains extremely busy running the school, he or she will guide you through part of, if not the entire ex-missions process. Your meetings with your director will run smoothly if they are stress free and upbeat.

Between running the school, meeting with many families, including current families who are not applying out, the last thing your director wants to deal with is controversy. Since his/her time to meet with you is limited, every second counts. Come prepared with a list of questions or concerns. Leave the complaints behind!

Your director communicates with the ongoing admission directors. You want these conversations to be positive and you want your family presented in the best possible light!

Nursery School Directors Must Be Honest

Directors have their own reputations to preserve. They are in charge of getting your child into a school, as well as the thousands of children that come after yours. It is important for them to convey a positive, yet honest, picture of your family. If you were the kind of family that "hovered" over every move a teacher made or questioned every school policy or complained at every turn, your director cannot say, "This family will make your staff appreciate coming to work every day ..." They must tell the truth about the families and children they represent or they will lose their credibility with their colleagues. Ongoing schools are wary of overbearing parents. While they appreciate parents who are actively involved in the school, the ones who spend 24/7 in their child's school will pose a red flag.

Nursery school directors will try to convey this aspect of your behavior in a diplomatic manner, but they have to be honest at the same time. Once a director's reputation is tarnished or an on-going school feels that the director has not been forthcoming, the trust in that director's word is greatly diminished. This would be terribly unfair to the families that follow at the school in the ongoing years.

Some candid pieces of advice when dealing when dealing with your school's professionals:

- Try not to be the center of attention!
- Do your best to get along with the director.
- Always be diplomatic.

Your involvement in the school can be highlighted through some common sense behavior on your part such as: monetary contributions to the annual fund, donating books to the school library, making cookies for the bake sale or volunteering for a teacher appreciation event.

What Can We Do To Empower Ourselves?

Schedule a meeting with your director in late summer or early September of the year you are applying to an on-going school. At that time you and your director will create a list of appropriate schools for your child. Come prepared with a list of thoughtful questions, revealing that you have done your homework on the subject of ongoing schools.

However you feel, maintain the approach that the director is the expert in the process and you are seeking his or her advice. Don't be argumentative or persistent about your needs or those of your child. Express your desires clearly, but nicely, and present yourself and your child's achievements with humility and modesty.

You will be encouraged to add 'safety' schools to your list. Follow these suggestions! Safety schools are not bad schools. While they may not be your first choice, they may have more available spaces. In our experience, having at least two safety schools on your list can improve your chance of securing a spot and they may actually surprise you by turning out to be the best fit for your child.

The ISAAGNY Report

Nursery schools are required to complete an ISAAGNY (Independent Schools Admissions Association of Greater New York) approved school report that is submitted to all the schools to which your child applies.

This report provides a comprehensive description of your child's important developments: social/emotional, physical, verbal skills, understanding of mathematical concepts, pre-reading skills, and… your involvement in the school.

While these reports are confidential, you are allowed to ask the director if any "negative attributes" will be mentioned in the report. This information will help you prepare for any related questions that might arise during your interviews. Make sure you have fulfilled all your financial commitments (tuition payments) as promptly as you possibly can. This is also cited in the report and can come back to haunt you if you have made late payments.

Not The Nursery School Director's Job!

Their job is NOT to offer "bribes/ gifts" on your behalf to ongoing schools! (Trust us ... we've been given flowers and offered a free stay at a five-bedroom apartment overlooking the river Seine in Paris. This behavior always backfires on parents!) They may communicate your family lineage or contributions to MOMA, but they cannot lie to a school to secure a spot for your child.

The nursery school director serves as a facilitator and guide in this process. He or she is NOT a guarantor or a crusader. His or her experience and years of goodwill with the ongoing schools may provide an edge over amateur directors or newer schools with less of a track record, but they cannot guarantee a spot in your top choice school.

So, please, be nice to your nursery school director! Know that they have a difficult job and want this process to work out best for all their families. If you do your homework to help the process along, you'll create a smoother working relationship. That's your goal.

4

The New York City metropolitan area offers hundreds of excellent educational choices. Some of the oldest most respected private schools in the country are located in your city. An amazing aspect of living in New York City is the opportunity afforded to parents who have the privilege of applying their kids to a wide array of top-notch independent schools.

Along with this privilege comes the responsibility of learning how to "play the admissions game" New York Style! And that is what we are here to guide you and your child through.

You may learn that there are too many terrific schools from which to choose, as opposed to not enough! Many families often begin their school search with the assumption that they know the best fit for their children. But, inevitably, they are in for a surprise. We have advised you before, and do so again — keep an open mind when looking at schools.

The schools have embraced New York City's "melting pot" of cultures. You will discover that each school has a unique personality, culture and style. The good news is that most families will relate to the cultures of many schools, not just one. I visited a range of traditional to very progressive schools for my daughter and discovered that many different philosophies resonated with my family values, as well as my daughter's needs. My choices became ones that made the most sense for our family. For example, it was very important to our family that we have both our kids in the same school and that they would have access to a campus environment.

Use these suggestions to narrow your choices

Prior to visiting schools, think about the "ideal" educational environment for your family. (This may change as you complete tours and realize the range of schools and options that are out there.)

Ask yourself the following questions with regard to your child's needs:

Do you want a small or a large school?

Would you be comfortable in a traditional or progressive setting?

Do you prefer single sex or co-ed?

Which special subject areas are important to your family? Examples are: physical education, movement, science, foreign languages, art, library, and woodworking.

Are these same subjects an important part of the schools' curriculum? How are they integrated?

What do you value most? Community service, diversity, academics, social/emotional development? I knew at the beginning of my school search that I wanted a school that valued more than academics. Physical activities, recess time, and movement were just as important to my husband and me as reading, writing, and math. We knew we wanted a school that placed a high value on ethics and community building. These come in many forms and a number of schools resonated with us on this level. There were also many schools that did not incorporate these values in the way that was important to us. We eliminated them from our list early on.

Special Needs Schools

It is difficult to know if your child has or will have special learning needs in the early years. If you already know this, then you are fortunate to be one step ahead of the process. You can focus on schools that cater to those needs. There are both special need schools as well as schools that mainstream children with special needs in their regular classrooms. Do your research. Tour both types of schools to ascertain which might be the best fit for your child's specific needs as well as your families' values. Categorize your school list under three headings:

- WHAT you KNOW about schools
- WHAT you WOULD LIKE to KNOW
- WHAT you have LEARNED

We offer a sample of this chart in the appendices. List all the schools to which you are applying. Now think about the headings above and make your notes.

This might sound like a lot of work, but after touring and interviewing at ten different schools, it all becomes a big blur. Notes and this visual list will help keep your thoughts clear and contribute to an easier decision process.

Your list will provide visual data of the schools. You can then sub-categorize this data into pros and cons that will enable you to narrow your list from ten to potentially three or four schools that can serve as your top choices. Share this list with your nursery school director.

My husband and I started our school tours with a preconceived notion on what we wanted and thought would work best for our son. We came from a very traditional, single-sex school setting and gravitated towards these attributes. We wanted a school with strong academics, uniforms, children sitting in desks, and silence in the hallways. We thought that 'progressive education' was a loosey/goosey, crunchy granola setting where children ran around the hallways doing whatever they pleased. We were so wrong!

New Schools

A whole crop of new ongoing schools have been introduced to the NYC private school landscape. Educators have assessed, analyzed and acknowledged the ever-changing needs and demands of parents and schools alike. They are also addressing the problem of too many kids and just not enough schools. The newer schools have developed their own philosophy of education with the aim to achieve high academic standards along with maintaining a variety of educational choices and values.

For example, some schools have felt the importance of a second language in the global economy. These schools have introduced a bilingual immersion program. Some feel that progressive education hasn't received its due credit. They have incorporated the positives of many of the top progressive schools in the city to start their own vision. There are also schools catering primarily to "gifted" children. These schools realize that parents want a space for their children who are primarily focused on academic achievements and do not want to be a part of the public school setting.

Basic Facts about Independent Schools
(This information is taken directly from the ISAAGNY & NYSAIS websites)

Independent schools are directly accountable to parents. This influences both structure and services. Most of the New York City independent schools are accredited with NYSAIS (New York State Association of Independent Schools) and are ISAAGNY Member Schools (Independent Schools Admission Association of Greater New York). The schools are compelled to follow strict guidelines for admissions and maintain certain standards of educational quality and staff competence.

ISAAGNY member schools admit students of any race, color, national or ethnic origin to all the rights and privileges, programs and activities generally accorded or made available to students at their schools. They do not discriminate on the basis of race, color, sexual preference, national or ethnic origin in administration of their educational policies, admissions policies, scholarships and loan programs, and athletic and other school-administered programs.

Currently there are 127 member schools. 67 of these schools are ongoing schools. 60 are preschools. There are 10 special education schools. For more information, visit the ISAAGNY Website: www.isaagny. org.

Our amazing city offers a wide array of schools that identify with their neighborhood and location. There is a school for every kind of family.

How Will We Know If This Is The Right School For Our Family?

Once you've toured all your schools and your chart is completed, schedule your interview dates. (Some schools automatically schedule these dates after your application is entered into their database)

This is the time to narrow or amend your list. Add schools to your top three or eliminate the ones that no longer appeal to you. You will have a clear feeling of schools that resonated with you. It's a combination of your research, homework, and instinctive reactions. You will walk into certain schools and feel like you are home. It's karmic.

Some of your pre-conceived notions will be what you expected, some will be tossed out the window. Be open and ready for some delightful surprises!

I recently attended a parent information session at an elite girls' school for my own child, and knew right off the bat that this was not a good fit.

The first giveaway was that every parent was only interested in where my daughter attended pre-school. Pretty soon I started saying a very well-known preschool, where my daughter didn't attend, in order to avoid their looks of confusion and disapproval!

The second sign was that when all the moms sat in a straight row of chairs during the admission director's presentation, my legs were the only ones encased in black hose. Every single other woman in the room was wearing nude hose. Obviously, I hadn't gotten the memo! But that subtle cue told me that this would not be the right place for our family.

5

Top Tier Schools – A Myth?

Parents want their children to attend the best schools – schools with the most sterling reputations. The brand names.

It is a perfectly natural desire to want to help ensure a path to success. A number of parents believe that this path begins with preschool, thinking:

If my child gets into the best pre-school, they will surely get into the top on-going school (where they will make the highest quality friends), which will ensure their best chance of getting into the top college which will put them on the path to a bright and successful future.

Really? So that's how it works?

We think it is more important for you to aspire to get your child into a great nursery school that is an excellent fit for your child at this point in time. You should not be thinking about bragging rights or future colleges!

Pre-school represents a child's first formal exposure to an environment which emphasizes collaboration, daily structure, learning to listen to other adults, and being away from mom and dad for at least two to three hours a day. Your child should look forward to going to "school" each morning to see his teachers and friends and to learn new ideas.

This eagerness will translate into a love of learning. That is why the first school experience should be a positive one and as perfect a fit for your child as possible. If you are raising a child that loves learning and loves attending school, he will be more successful in adapting to academic challenges as he grows older.

From this solid foundation you will learn more about your child's personality—his/her needs both socially and academically. In cooperation with your nursery school teachers and director, you will be able to identify the best on-going schools to meet the needs of your child.

Again, we strongly emphasize that this endeavor is not about bragging rights. All New York independent private schools offer fabulous educations. All are concerned with each child's well-being, both socially and academically. All educators want to do right by the child and his parents, and all are just as concerned about preparing a child for future success, as are the parents.

Here's What We Think

If you are only applying to what everyone believes is the top-tier nursery school, in hopes of getting your child into a top on-going school, do you think you are alone with that idea? Nope. In New York City, many highly competitive families would use that same thought process.

That means many families from your hypothetical nursery school will be applying to the same on-going schools in which you want your child to attend. Therefore, your opportunity to be accepted to an on-going school of your choice might just actually increase if your child is coming from a less "popular" pre-school, but one that still offers a solid foundation/preparation for Pre-K or Kindergarten.

You should not be concerned with status, which is what is really conveyed by the term "top-tier." Rather, always be concerned with finding the right fit for your child. This is an important consideration for ensuring your child's successful future. There are no guarantees in life, despite our wishes for them. And remember, there is more than one school that will offer an excellent fit.

6

Standardized Tests…
Then and Now!

I was told that my child must take a standardized test as part of the admissions process. I heard that some schools use a test for kindergarten and some don't. Is this true?

This is true... as of now. Previously, ERB tests were required by schools as part of the admissions process for Kindergarten and 1st Grades. Currently, New York City independent schools are not using the ERB, but some schools are using other tests to help them obtain a fuller understanding of an applicant's abilities.

The ERB test has been used for the past fifteen years. This valuable tool was used to help schools obtain an assessment of a student's strengths and weaknesses. Unfortunately, the ERB has been compromised and is no longer a fair assessment of a child's abilities.

Parents were able to purchase this test (for a steep price). Too many children were being prepped for the test, which, of course, produced unreliable results. The value of the information was diminished by the test preparation and also resulted in a lack of identification of learning differences or specific weaknesses. So while a child might present with significant strengths in some areas, the inability to identify the weaknesses meant that appropriate professionals would not address these areas.

The ERB offered useful information as part of the complex puzzle for evaluating all candidates. The scores and their consistency were noted, along with the comprehensive write-up provided by the ERB tester. This written evaluation, matched with what admissions associates observed in playgroup as well as the information offered in the nursery school report, proved helpful in admissions decisions. If the written evaluations did not match what was observed by the admissions staff, this served as a clue that something was amiss and required further investigation. Without the ERB data, admissions directors could only rely on their own playgroup/child interview and the nursery school report.

Schools recognize that a uniform method in assessing applicants is necessary. This is being addressed for Kindergarten.

The latest test to be given to kindergarten applicants for some of the NYC private schools is the Admissions Test for Beginning Learners® (AABL® test). This is an iPad-administered, child-friendly assessment of a child's development in the areas of verbal and quantitative reasoning, early literacy and mathematics skills. National experts in these fields developed the AABL for Pre-Kindergarten through Grade 1. In development since 2011, the AABL has been extensively field-tested. Some schools require this test. Others rely on their own "evaluations" during the child's school visit.

The Admissions Test for Beginning Learners or AABL test is administered by the ERB (Educational Records Bureau). Schools can arrange to become test sites, so this test may be offered at your child's preschool. Trained professionals administer the test to students one-on-one or in small groups. Because the test is performed on an iPad, we recommend that children have experience using an iPad before taking this test.

Unlike the old ERB test, which was an IQ test assessing intellectual abilities, the AABL test is a readiness (achievement-type) test covering "verbal and quantitative reasoning, early literacy, and mathematics." Skills in phonics, pre-reading, and math are measured. These skills were not evaluated on the ERB test.

*The ECAA for Grades 2-4

The Early Childhood Admissions Assessment (ECAA) administered by the Education Records Bureau (ERB) is an assessment for students applying to 2nd through 4th grades. It is used as an admissions tool at some private elementary schools across the country. Students may take the test only once during a given admissions season.

The ECAA (ERB adapted WISC-IV) for application to Grade 2 features 10 unique subtests. Five of these subtests explore verbal skills and five of these subtests measure non-verbal abilities. Overall, the scores on these subtests may be combined to yield one full scale composite score.

The ECAA (ERB adapted WISC-IV & CTP – Reading Comprehension) for application to Grades

3-4 features 10 unique subtests from the WISC-IV (as stated above) as well as a Reading Comprehension assessment.

More information on the ECAA can be obtained on the ERB website www.erblearn.org

*ISEE

The Independent School Entrance Exam (ISEE) is an entrance exam for private middle and high schools administered by the Educational Records Bureau (ERB). There are three versions of the test:

1. Lower Level (LL) for students applying to Grades 5 and 6.
2. Middle Level (ML) for students applying to Grades 7 and 8.
3. Upper level (UL) for students applying to Grades 9 - 12.

Each version has questions in verbal reasoning, quantitative reasoning, reading comprehension mathematical achievement, and a writing sample.

The ISEE is a standard assessment of skills for each applicant, ranking his or her reasoning and achievement skills among students in the same grade. It enables students to take a single, fair, and reliable test for entrance into independent schools.

The ISEE, ECAA, and AABL can be taken once in each admission cycle.

What Can I Do To Prepare My Child for Kindergarten and for the AABL?

- Reading (vocabulary and comprehension)
- Mighty Minds, matching different shapes such as circles, squares, polygons, triangles to fit in different pictures (spatial relations)
- Brain Quest Cards (logic)
- Mazes
- Workbooks (fine motor, logic)
- Drawing (fine motor, creative thinking)
- Beading (fine motor)
- Patterning (what would come next)
- Copying shapes (fine motor, spatial)
- Conflict resolution (social judgment)
- Organizing food groups (categorizing)

Yikes! We Bombed!

Waiting for your test results can drive the best of us to drink … smoothies, we hope. Try to remain calm. Not all schools make judgments solely on high scores. If your child's scores are not what you had hoped for, you may need to rethink some of the schools on your list. This doesn't mean that your child will be rejected from all, but expanding your list may give your child more advantage.

Testing is a fact of life in the world of private school admissions. Try your best to accept the process and results, knowing that the more you learn about your child's strengths and weaknesses at an early age, the more you will be able to appropriately help your child to obtain the school experience in which he or she will thrive and be happy.

Isn't this, after all, what we all want for our children?

* ERB website: www.erblearn.org

7

Single Sex vs. Co-ed?
Here's Our Take...

The debate: A single sex school for your child or a co-ed school with boys and girls together in the same classrooms? What type of educational environment would work best for your child and family?

We have lived through this dilemma and explored all sides of this legitimate educational option and debate.

My partner, Vimmi and her husband attended single sex schools. They thought that their son's education should also follow that model (it worked out well for them.) They grew up with the belief that children, especially boys, learn best in a single–sex school structure because this limits distractions. They believed that an educational environment should comprise a serious, academically challenging, structured approach. They believed that boys mature later than girls, as their verbal skills are not as advanced as their female counterparts'. While boys do catch up in later years, the early years are crucial for establishing a strong academic foundation, and the best way to do this, they felt, was in a single-sex school.

Jennifer and her husband, however, attended co-ed schools. A single-sex environment felt different and unnatural to them. They wanted their children to experience the 'real world' in their educational life, a world where boys and girls play and work together, collaborating and learning as equals.

All of our children ended up in co-ed schools. We learned a lot about the benefits of single-sex and co-ed environments during our search for the "right" school for our individual families. Now we have a better understanding of both types of education!

Here's how one of our clients felt:

> *Our daughter is shy, modest, unassuming, and definitely into her dolls and pink ribbons. Her favorite stories are about princesses.*
>
> *She physically moves away from boys on the playground and from our friends' sons. We thought a single sex school would be the right choice, hoping that as she develops greater confidence with her girlfriends, she will internalize this confidence in such a way to enable her to befriend boys as she matures. In the meantime, at a single sex school, she will be free to be herself in all her innately feminine ways. That's our thinking. We hope we're making the right choice.*

Single-Sex Schools

Boys and girls learn differently, at a different pace, due to their social and physical differences. This is the mantra of many single-sex schools. They value the importance of educating boys and girls separately, based on their gender-specific needs.

Many studies reveal that girls do better without the boys. Girls will spend more time studying. (Hmmm… Wonder why?) And they consequently show increased confidence in subjects like math and computers.

Likewise, since boys differ in dexterity (writing, drawing) and cognitive development (tending to slower maturation) there is a big push by some educators for the all boy schools. Boys can feel less threatened when expressing themselves and will take more risks. They can develop deeper friendships without girls around. (Hmmm…wonder again?)

While it is true that most of the single- sex schools are traditional, academic, and teacher directed, it is also true that they have realized the value of building self-esteem, confidence and autonomy in children during those early educational years. Some of the single sex schools in NYC have reworked their curriculum to develop a more progressive approach in their lower schools.

Co-ed Schools

Co-ed schools can be progressive or traditional in their approach. Educators in co-ed schools believe that children learn best in an environment that reflects the world in which they live. Boys and girls need to learn how to work and play with one another beginning at an early age. After all, in today's world, where more women are actively engaged in the workforce, men and women will be working together in a variety of jobs. An early introduction to learning to work side by side provides a good model for success in school and in life.

It Is Important To Keep an Open Mind

Hmmm...where have we heard this rap before?

School philosophies have changed and as we said, some single-sex schools, while still retaining a more traditional approach, have added a progressive element to their style and teaching that makes them more appealing to some. It's important to recognize that some co-ed schools remain very traditional, which appeals to different kinds of students and families.

We strongly recommend that you check out both models. You might be very surprised at what you discover. While Jennifer's daughter and son are both in co-ed schools, she values all that an all-girls' school offers. She gave a great deal of consideration to what might be the best fit, especially for her daughter, and felt torn between both options. Jennifer is so conflicted that while both her kids attend co-ed schools, she sends her son to an all-boys' camp for the benefits of the single-sex approach.

Vimmi and her husband have grown to appreciate the advantages offered by a co-ed school. They have seen their son flourish and thrive in his school. While what they originally envisioned for their son was very different, in maintaining an open mind, they came to see the value, for him, in co-ed education.

The lesson here is to check out both types of schools; see what feels right and where you can envision your child and family. You may be surprised by what you learn!

Both theories have great validity, and the debate has been raging on for decades. There is no winning this debate! It comes down to weighing the pluses and minuses or the features and benefits for your unique children.

We applied to an *all boys'* school for our middle son. During the tour he said, "I have seen enough and I am leaving." He walked right out of the building.

The facial expressions of the admissions officers registered shock that a four-year-old boy would leave on his own in the middle of their tour! The school had no idea that our driver was waiting right outside.

We were so embarrassed. We said, "I guess that ends the interview." They agreed.

8

Summer Birthdays?
A Dilemma

My son was born in June, July, or August. He will have just turned five by the September 1st cut off for ongoing schools. What do I do?

Remember ongoing schools are the ones that you apply to after nursery schools. They can start in Pre-Kindergarten or Kindergarten and could end in 8th grade or 12th grade. There are a few schools that actually start in Nursery and end in 12th grade. These are few and far between.

I have heard that it is not good to be the youngest in the class. Should I apply to ongoing schools or should I wait another year?

This is an unresolved debate regarding social/academic and/or physical maturity and school readiness. If you examine the relevant studies, you won't find much.

Here's how one of our clients described her son:

All we hear about in the New York private school scene is that boys with summer birthdays are at a disadvantage. Yet our son, born in early August, is more mature than many of his playmates. He is a true companion to his friends, playing and sharing quite nicely.

His language skills are incredible. We need to find a way to convey this to the private schools so they can look at him without the prejudicial lens of summer birthdays.

Birthday Cut-off Dates

Most New York City ongoing schools use September 1st as their age cut-off date. A child applying for kindergarten must turn five on or before September 1st of the entry year.

Some schools are very strict about this date. If they are five by September 1st, they must apply to kindergarten, even if the birthday is August 31st.

Others adhere to this same date while being more flexible about looking at the applicant's social/pre-academic skills and making an appropriate recommendation to parents based on their evaluation. Some schools send a 'too young' letter to families whose children are born in the summer months. Many of our friends, acquaintances and clients have gone through the process of receiving a 'too young' letter. It only means that the schools would be interested in seeing the child the following year when they have greater maturity. They feel that spending an additional year in the current preschool program can benefit the child and get them ready for a formal ongoing school curriculum.

Many parents believe in holding summer birthday children back by having them begin kindergarten when they turn six. This is called redshirting.

Redshirt vs. Holding a Child Back For an Extra Year in Pre-K or Nursery School before Admitting Into Kindergarten

The term redshirting originally referred to postponing a college athlete's participation in regular season games for one year to give him an extra year of further growth and practice with the team in the hope of improving the player's skills for future seasons (see ERIC, Educational Resources Information Center).

Should We Apply or Hold Back?

To apply or not to apply...a difficult decision.

If your child has a summer birthday, take an honest, loving look at him. Your nursery school directors will also offer you guidance based on their experience with your child. Do you have reasons to believe that kindergarten will be overwhelming for him? If so, wait.

I tried to hold my son back (August 20th birthday) despite his higher than average height and excellent pre-academic skills. I felt he would benefit socially if he was an older boy in the classroom as opposed to the youngest in the grade. Personally, I do believe that most boys with a summer birthday should be held back. However, the school that I felt was the best fit for my son and family, after spending time with him and evaluating his application material, believed he would be just fine in the grade that reflected his birth

81

date. This was despite the fact that he would be the youngest in his class as opposed to the oldest.

The school will most likely have the final say in this matter though it is a beneficial conversation to have with your nursery school director and with the schools to which you are applying. If you feel, he will be able to succeed, both socially and academically, with children who could be one full year older, then you have no reason to delay the application process.

You will need to make a case for this in the essay section of your application. Be very clear about your rationale, citing examples to make your point. For example, you can stress your child's maturity to push ahead or his or her "need" for an extra year in pre-school to hold back. You can also draw on conversations you've had with your nursery school director and convey them in your respective essays. But also let the school know that you are open to their feedback and recommendations.

Make sure your nursery school director is on board with your decision. Schedule a meeting with your nursery school director to review schools that prefer holding a summer birthday child back, as well as the ones in which you need to apply to the grade which reflects his birthday.

You can call or e-mail the Director of Admissions to inquire how he or she handles summer birthdays. However, be informed because some schools will tell you to hold back while other schools really look at the birth date as their cut-off. If you make the decision to hold your child back, and to keep him/ her in his/her current nursery school for the equivalent of a kindergarten year, you might be applying your child to first grade the following year as opposed to kindergarten!

It is important to understand that just because you want to hold your child back, if they make the school cut-off for kindergarten, it is the ongoing school's final decision to which grade you may apply.

Note: There are very few first grade spots at any school.

9

OK, I Know Where to Apply... Now What?

Now it is time to request applications. This part of the process is straightforward. It used to be a challenge to obtain an application from your coveted school. The day following Labor Day consisted of a frenzy of phone calls to request applications. Parents found themselves dialing and redialing the admissions office, just for the privilege of requesting an application to an on-going school.

This part of the process is now far more simplified and humane!

Nursery Schools

Each nursery school has its own protocol. Many have started accepting on-line application requests in early August, a welcome relief to frustrated parents.

But some schools still need to be contacted via the traditional method-by phone the Tuesday after Labor Day (have your in-laws, parents, assistants plastered to the phones, calling schools simultaneously with you). Make sure everyone calling has access to your child's correct name, birth date, your address, telephone number as well as your calendar in case the schools want to schedule a meeting with you right away.

Some schools have made it easier by accepting application requests during the week following Labor Day (Tuesday thru Friday) and some nursery schools have introduced a lottery system. A random group of applicants are handpicked from the pool and notified a couple of weeks later via e-mail or postal mail. These schools will also collect all the information pertaining to you and your child during the week following Labor Day. If you get lucky and receive an application, fill it out and return it immediately. Unfortunately, if you do not make it through the lottery, you will not be able to apply for that year.

On-Going Schools

Most on-going schools now offer their applications on-line, posted in late August. You can submit the application online or download it, fill it out, and mail it to the school. Don't wait until the deadline!

Few schools ask you to fill out an inquiry on-line. They will mail you an application containing all the admissions information.

Another option is to stop by the school's admissions office and pick up the application materials. This, however, can be very time-consuming. Remember, most on-going school applications are available online and there really is no benefit to picking them up unless you like to physically get all your materials. But don't linger—ask for the application packet, thank them, and move on. There is no reason to get on their radar this early in the process.

We will never forget a parent who stopped by our former admissions office to get an application and wouldn't leave. This dad asked every possible question about the school before he even read any of the materials. It is very important to understand that the admissions office is not a place to stop by unannounced with a million questions. Please always call and schedule an appointment.

Very few schools require the completed application the day after Labor Day in order to obtain an interview spot, so don't panic.

We do suggest that you complete and submit the applications within the first month of the admission season, which does begin the day after Labor Day. Submitting the application early in the process ensures enough time to reschedule your child's visit or your school tour in case of an emergency or an illness.

Be sure to check the school's website for their application procedures by late August. By then, you should have completed your research and compiled a list of schools that are a good match for your family.

Financial Aid

Every application includes a box to place a checkmark in that says, "requesting financial aid." This box should be checked only if you are a family in genuine need of financial educational assistance.

Financial aid is not for families that can afford the tuition but might have to give up the luxury of a family ski trip to Aspen or summering in the Hamptons. Many wonderful families need assistance. There is no stigma attached to requesting financial aid. Schools are more than happy to help if they can, but keep in mind that they may not be able to grant full tuition assistance. They offer what they feel is appropriate on a case-by-case basis.

If you are seeking aid, it is critical that you submit your necessary paper work by the dates indicated on the forms you will receive.

Important Points

- Check each school's admissions procedure via their website
- Start a detailed filing system for each school you are interested in
- Most applications are available online
- Note each application deadline but apply early
- Note open house dates
- Write a first draft of your essays
- Complete applications by early October
- Save copies for your records

My husband and I were really looking forward to visiting this particular school, which happened to also be one of our top choices.

I thought my organizational skills were as perfect as they could be. I had an Excel spreadsheet of all our tour dates, a checklist of questions and comments to say on our tours, dress code for each school etc. Well, I messed up big time!

I went to the school for my child's interview... my son in tow. I did not realize that it was a date set up only for the parent's tour!

We made sure that our son was well rested the night before, he missed his school the day of our visit, ate a healthy breakfast and was ready to spend the day with mommy. It all went waste due to my mistake. This was so embarrassing!

Moral of the story: Over organization is not always a guarantee for success. Thank goodness the school had a sense of humor and we ended up getting accepted there anyway!

10

Essays Don't Have To Do You In!

We have read thousands of private school application essays. We've laughed, we've cried, we've slept through many.

A good application essay should be concise, personal, and memorable. The following tips will ensure that you will compose a great essay.

I have so much to say. I could actually write a book.

Please, write a book…then give it to the grandparents or save it for your memoir! The essay about your child, however, should not be longer than one page. The admissions staff reads hundreds of essays during the season. Admissions officers are interested and do want to learn more about your child, however, they want to learn more about your child in one page, not five or ten!

Choose four or five adjectives that describe your child. Then write your essay and support the top two or three with succinct personal anecdotes. The anecdotes should reflect your child and family in a positive light. You can be funny, silly, quirky, and honest. Just keep it real and your child's personality will shine through.

Keep It Personal

The essays that will stand out have the most personal and interesting anecdotes about your child and your family. Watch how your child interacts with others and note the unique things he does on a regular basis. Will your child's personality add to the school environment? How?

The essays provide a unique opportunity to reflect on your child's special personality.

I remember tearing up as I wrote about my daughter's determination to swim. It was very touching to me, and revealed a lot about who she is as a person. Use these personal moments to bring your child to life on the page.

The essays should be well written and grammatically correct. You don't need to be a professional writer to reveal your fabulous child. Computers offer spelling and grammar checks. Use them! You want the admissions professionals to be touched and gratified that you took your time to present a well-written and thoughtful essay.

If you are not confident in your writing skills, do the best you can and then have a trusted friend (who is also an excellent writer) look it over and get his/her valued opinion. If it is not polished enough, go back and do it over until you are comfortable with it. This is important so don't rush it at the last minute.

Do Not Highlight Your Child's Weaknesses

Weaknesses? What weaknesses? Well, yes, every child has a few. But the application essay is not the place to highlight temper tantrums, or how he hits his sibling, or every time he has told you, "You are the worst mommy ever!"

Your goal is to portray a realistic and loving view of your child's personality. Admissions staff will meet your child and be able to see his or her attributes for themselves, so it's important to be honest and believable.

However, it is just as important not to hide things that a school needs to know. Most schools will offer a parent interview or a space on the application for additional information. This is the place or time to offer a fuller explanation of any physical limitations, a trauma in the child's life with which he/she is coping, or allergies, etc. These are not weaknesses, but rather critical information that will assist the admissions office and you in finding the proper fit for your family. So, while you will not write about every meltdown, do not hide vital information that would be detrimental to your child or the school if the school did not know about it.

One of our client's children had a physical impairment that made it very difficult for him to walk up and down steps. This kind of impairment would need to be discussed in an essay to make sure that the school could accommodate this child's needs. Likewise, if a child has a major illness (juvenile diabetes, leukemia, etc.) that affects his/her daily life, this should also be mentioned in the essay.

Clarify Your Affinity for the School

Think seriously about why you have chosen to apply to a particular school. The admissions office is seeking a great fit between the school and your family. Become familiar with each school's educational philosophy.

Is their philosophy a good fit for your family? Does the school's mission statement reflect your family's values? Do you seek a single sex school? Why? Are sports your main focus or does academics rule?

Be honest with yourself and the admissions staff!

It is important to understand why you believe that a particular school or two would be the best fit for you and your child. You must be able to articulate this in your own words.

We suggest taking mental (or written) notes while touring the school. Jot down important observations immediately after your tour. Incorporate them in your essay. These notes, plus those from the open houses, will be helpful in credibly communicating your strong interest in the school. DO NOT simply replicate the words of the school's mission statement. Trust us! Admission readers recognize their own words in print.

The key is to carefully read what the mission

statement is telling you about the school's priorities. Do they really match your priorities or are you just impressed with the school's reputation regardless of the fit with your child?

For my family, academics were highly important when looking at a school. Another aspect that was of high value was community service. I applied to schools that incorporated both high academic standards as well as 'giving back' to the community into their curriculum.

After thinking about what is most important to you in relation to what the school offers, be sure to prominently mention that in your essay. Be specific and credible about how these values are already incorporated into your daily life.

Additional Information, Please

If a school's application offers the opportunity to provide additional information, do not reiterate what you've already written. There are no brownie points for filling up the entire essay portion. Only provide additional information that will help the school better understand your family and child.

One of our clients used this space to carefully describe the death of his or her spouse and how they are helping his or her child understand and accept this situation. This was appropriate and helpful. It is important for a school to know this information to better assist you and your child adjust to a new school environment.

This is not the space, however, to divulge your family's deep dark secrets like the long lost uncle who was arrested last year or the voices you hear at night!

An application essay should be a snapshot of:

- Your child's personality
- Your family
- The compatibility of your values with the school's values

Warning:

Double check if you mention the school's name in your essay and be sure it's in the correct envelope correlating to that school.

Lastly, picture an overwhelmed admissions officer reading hundreds and hundreds of essays. Yours should be that outstanding essay that remains with the reader for some time!

ESSAYS DO's AND DON'Ts

- Do make the essay about your child no longer than a single page.

- Do pick four or five adjectives that describe your child and support them with personal anecdotes.

- Do make your essay well written and grammatically correct.

- Do reflect the true personality of your child in your essay.

- Do have a trusted friend or close family member read your essay if you are unsure of your writing abilities.

- **Don't** use language that highlights your child's 'weaknesses'.

- **Don't** just copy from the school's materials for your essay. Why has your family applied to this particular school? Communicate the reasons in your own words.

- **Don't** reiterate what is already mentioned in the original essay if a school's application gives the opportunity to provide additional information.

My daughter asked the teacher during her playgroup visit: "When are we going to the playground?"

She must have felt like she was already accepted and in her future classroom- she was that comfortable!

11

Tips for Your Child's Playgroup/ Interview

How will my child behave? What if he throws a fit? What if he/she doesn't look the interviewer in the eye or clings to my leg, refusing to go with the other children?

Most parents worry about their children's response to the playgroup visit. The parents' calm, cool exterior is often an attempt to mask their own doubts about how their child will react. You are not alone in feeling nervous!

Admissions professionals are just that… professionals! They are trained to recognize the many moods and behaviors of children. We all hope (pray) our children are demonstrating their perfect, adorable, smart, sweet, and ever so precious sides at this important meeting, but let's get real. They are babies, or four years of age. Their moods can change like the wind. We have seen everything from children screaming hysterically, hitting their parents, to even wetting their pants.

During one playgroup we witnessed a child screaming outside the door, "I want to go home" as loud as he could. No one could console this child and his parents stood there looking helpless. Finally, they asked an admissions person in the room if they could leave the room to calm him down. They left with the boy, only to return five minutes later. The boy was quiet for a little while and then started screaming again! They left the room for good, we are sure, completely embarrassed.

During another playgroup, there was a little girl

crying. Her nose was running and the mother didn't have a tissue. She was trying to hide her daughter's tears while wiping her nose with her hand. It was terribly humiliating for her (and painful for us to witness).

Do not put additional stress on your child by revealing how stressed you are. Maintain your calm and reassuring demeanor at all times.

I will never forget struggling with my daughter in an interview, prying her fingers off my leg, smiling and laughing, while dying inside. We cannot predict or do much about how our children will act. But we can control how we react and walk into these stressful situations with a well thought out plan which we will describe below.

Be Your Child's Advocate

Yelling or coercion does not work. If your child will not separate from you and join the group, all eyes will be on the actions of you and your spouse. Do not say the usual things like, "He never does this" or "I don't know what's wrong with him." Don't make any lame, trite excuses! Simply reassure your child and take your cues from the admissions staff. Let them take the lead. Listen to their advice. They see this all the time and are used to negotiating with children. Their observations on how you react can serve to help (or hurt) his/her overall prospects for admission.

For example, if you begin to yell and scream at

your child or spouse, it will be noted in a negative way. Admissions staff likes to see calm, positive and thoughtful resolutions to problems. Always remember there are good days and bad days. Some days we come undone and some days we can hold it together. In this unpredictable, stressful process parents strive to do their best, recognizing that they are being assessed as well.

Use these sound tips to ensure that the "sweet, yummy" and wonderful side of your child also shines through.

When Should I Get To The Interview?

Arrive at the interview early, but not too early. Getting to the school about 10 minutes early will give your child plenty of time to take in the new setting and get comfortable. There may be books or paper and crayons to keep him/her entertained. Reading a book or drawing together can be very calming for a child prior to this sort of meeting.

If you arrive too early, you inadvertently provide the opportunity for your child to become restless or anxious, or worse to start tearing the artwork off the walls.

Timing can be challenging due to traffic or not being familiar with a new neighborhood. If you plan to leave extra early to ensure your timely arrival for the playgroup/interview, it will be helpful to bring something that is a sure hit with your child. Make sure, though, it is something the child can easily leave behind once they are called to join the playgroup!

Some things that have worked are: a favorite storybook, mini activity book or any transitional object to which they can easily say goodbye.

Do not bring anything that is electronic, buzzes, beeps or rings loudly!

Dress Up Or Dress Down?

Dressing your child each morning can be one of the more challenging tasks parents experience. I must confess, somehow there were times when my children wore some part of their pajamas to school!

Try to select the school outfit the night before in order to make the morning go smoothly. Dress your child appropriately for the schools to which you are applying…yet remain flexible.

Avoid jeans when visiting a traditional school; similarly, avoid formal attire when visiting a progressive school. Your child should feel comfortable. If he/she really wants to wear shoes that don't exactly match their outfit, just go with it! (Progressive schools might enjoy this creative out-of-the-box attire).

I Gotta Pee Pee!

This is one of the most important things you can do for your child and for the admissions staff!

TAKE YOUR CHILD TO THE BATHROOM ONCE THEY ARRIVE AT SCHOOL or just before they leave home, even if they convincingly say, "I don't have to go." A bathroom break during playgroup time can be disruptive. It is also hard to get a good sense of a child if he spends a portion of their playgroup time in the bathroom stall.

My Child Is Sick! What Do I Do?

Let us be clear and concise: Stay Home!

It is challenging to get all your playgroups/ tours/ interviews planned. It is equally hard to coordinate your schedule, your spouse's schedule, and your child's busy schedule. We get it! It's disappointing when, after all that effort and planning; your child starts vomiting at night or awakes with a fever.

We understand that these interviews are difficult to reschedule, but a child is never at his/her best when sick. (It is also unfair to the other children and the interviewers).

Call the school as soon as you realize your child is ill and let the school know he/she is too sick to make the appointment. The school will understand.

Do I Tell My Child What To Do During Playgroup?

I will never forget a boy who built a high tower with blocks. He kept building and building. He was so focused and determined. When the admissions staff member asked what he was building, he replied, "I don't know, my mommy told me to just build a super high tower." So many children have also told us that their mommy will buy them a present if they're really good today!

We observe children saying these things too often! Do not tell your child what to do or how to act. This backfires. Can you imagine what goes through the admissions persons' minds when they hear a child confessing that he/she was instructed by his/her parents to behave a certain way at the playgroup or at an interview?

However, good manners are important. It is okay to ask your child to be polite, to look at the teacher when asked questions and…A smile goes a long way!

Let your children be themselves. Their true personalities usually appear. The admissions teams are trained educators and are usually great at uncovering a child's true personality. Which can be good…or not so good for some.

Last, But Not Least…

Lighten up! Take a deep breath. A nervous parent always brings out the nervousness in a child!

PLAYGROUP INTERVIEW
DO'S and DON'Ts

- Do arrive early, but not too early.

- Do dress your child appropriately for the schools to which you are applying…yet remain flexible.

- Do take your child to the bathroom prior to the playgroup/interview.

- Do refrain from coaching your children on "how to act." Let them be themselves…their true personalities usually appear.

- Do stay calm, relaxed and positive!

- **Don't** bring a sick child to a playgroup.

I learned the hard way that when schools tell you to, "dress casually," for an interview, they do not mean come in work-out clothes from the gym!

My daughter had a weekend playgroup. I was very new to this process and really did not know much about the schools. I asked how I should dress for a Saturday morning playgroup (at this very traditional single-sex school). I was told to dress casually and to put my daughter in "play-clothes."

Well, my idea of casual and the school's idea of casual were very different!

There I sat, in my gym clothes, while everyone else was in nice pants, sweaters, the men even wore jackets! I felt like an idiot!

We then had a discussion with the teachers who also wore heels and were impeccably dressed! Thank goodness my daughter had better instincts than I did and insisted on wearing a "twirly skirt" that morning!

12

Tips for Middle/High School Interviews

You are never fully dressed without a smile!

This age old saying has never been truer than when you are interviewing for a private school's class spot! We mean it! Arriving at an interview with a smile on your face makes a great first impression as you greet the admissions staff.

The individual who will chat with you has met with hundreds of applicants. Nothing is more welcoming to a busy interviewer than getting to know a happy, smiling candidate who is excited and ready to share information about themselves and prepared to express why they wish to be a part of a new school community!

Excitement Is Also Key!

It is not fun to interview someone who is half asleep or does not seem to want to be there. We know these interviews can be stressful and cause anxiety. Your goal is to develop rapport, be comfortable, and share interesting information. This will occur more naturally if you are genuinely excited by the new school. Excitement is revealed in many ways. Smile, look directly at the interviewer, and come prepared with interesting stories about yourself. This will convey that you really want one of the few available spots. The admissions interviewer will definitely note this.

Do Your Homework!

An applicant must do their homework to under-stand the school's attributes. This will illustrate your desire to be part of their community.

Mention:

- Specifics about the campus noted on the tour
- A special program the school offers or a specific class that seems interesting.

For example, a campus school offers on-site sports. If you are a sports enthusiast, this is an inviting subject to discuss. If the school has a new science lab and you love science, this is a great conversation starter! Find one or two aspects about the curriculum that especial-ly appeals to you.

Keep It Personal

Personal stories are the best way to keep an inter-view interesting. The admissions staff wants to like you and is seeking students who will add to a lively, diverse community. Think about the subjects for which you have passion, the personal stories you can share which illustrate who you are, and how you can add to their community. An interviewer will often say, "Tell me about yourself." Be prepared to share something that is key to who you are. One teenager we worked with loved basketball. He was on a very competitive team. He wanted to share this about himself and include the fact that he started his own tutoring program with underprivileged kids that came out of participation on his Basketball team. He had this in mind when he went into his interviews … we call this "having stories in your pocket."

No Negatives

If you are applying to middle or high School, you will be changing from one school to another. You may be asked about your current school. Keep anything said about the current school upbeat and positive! You may not have liked some things about your current school: teachers, some students, sports or lack of sports, too rigorous academics or not rigorous enough, your school felt too big or too small. It is better to focus on the good things about the school you are leaving as opposed to the negatives. Instead, express excitement to experience a new school with new friends!

Ask Questions

We encourage you to ask questions about the school but pose questions that are genuine, ones that are truly important to you. If you have had the chance to tour the school before the interview, this is a great time to think of a few questions about what you have observed. Other questions might involve sports teams, clubs, after school programs, the language program, and electives! Inquire about student government if this truly interests you.

REMEMBER...

- Think of your meeting with the admissions rep as a conversation. Admissions folks truly enjoy meeting prospective students.
- Smile and share your excitement to visit.
- Do your homework — understand the school's philosophy.
- Have personal "stories in your pocket" ready to share.
- Don't speak negatively about your current school.
- Ask questions, which are genuine.
- Try to relax and have fun.

13

Is My Child the Only One Being Interviewed…?

Although your child is a critical participant in the admissions process, he/she is not the sole factor in the school's decision. In fact, the parent interview is not limited to just one meeting with you. The admissions staff can and will informally note things about you and your family during your school tour, your child's visit and every interaction with you. Even your phone manners will be noted. (Yes, we know it is stressful to be aware of constantly being under a microscope. But just be happy, upbeat and positive!)

So you need to be on your best behavior at all times. We know there are days and times when children do not cooperate (gasp) or your spouse might get on your nerves (yep it happens to the best of us) or the admissions person is not that welcoming on the phone. Still, through it all, you must keep it all together and compose yourself.

Remember what you learned in elementary school? "Please" and "Thank you" are very important words. Be sure to use them! We are not talking about your kids here...we are referring to you and your spouse!

Giving everyone a chance to speak and truly listening to the person who is speaking to you is critical, especially when he or she is the one making the crucial decisions on your child's admission.

Five Tips to Help You through Your Interviews:

1) Be honest about your child's strengths, but do not exaggerate!

The interviewer wants to obtain a true glimpse of your child's personality and how he/she might contribute to the school community. We know it is hard not to brag about your wonderful child. We all love our special children. Rather than bragging, focus on your child's unique strengths and present them honestly, realistically, and with deserved pride. Remember, these people hear this same information over and over again from loving parents so try to be articulate and original.

For example when Vimmi described her own son, she spoke about his love for planets and space. She discussed that he was reading books about the solar system and incorporated them in his artwork. She used this example to illustrate how he was a self-motivated learner. This was not to brag, but it was factual and unique to her child. It also showed him in a positive light.

When parents present a "perfect" child, a child too wonderful, it becomes "too wonderful" to believe.

A couple I know once described the altruistic side of their daughter, which mirrored the behavior of a Saint.

"Our daughter is so selfless, that she would rather give her cookies to a homeless person, than eat them herself."

The child was very sweet, but it is next to impossible for a four year old to live up to so much praise.

Remember: the children will spend a considerable amount of quality time with admission professionals so offer a positive, but realistic picture! Don't build your child up to the point where the interviewer has such high expectations that your son/daughter does not live up to your introduction! This will cause the admissions officers to wonder if everything else you've told them was also equally exaggerated.

2) *Turn off your smartphones/iPad/etc. Free your mind of work-related projects so you can focus on the moment.*

We cannot state this more emphatically. Talking on your cell phone, emailing clients or friends, texting or replying to someone during a tour or interview is totally unacceptable. It looks bad, it is bad, and it is disrespectful. Just Don't Do It!

We actually ask our clients to leave their phones at home or turn them off when they are in a scheduled admissions meeting with a school.

I had one dad excuse himself to answer his phone in the middle of a parent admissions interview. He had a full conversation before he hung up. He looked at me, (as if it wasn't the rudest moment of his life) and said, "Go on"…

That example occurs infrequently. However, once is enough. Refrain from using your phone. If there is a true potential emergency, and no one can cover for you during your visit, explain the situation to the interviewer or tour guide prior to the tour or interview.

We know this process takes a lot out of your busy schedules but, if done with real focus and conviction, you will greatly improve your child's chances of admission.

3) *Always show respect for, and a united front with your co-parent.*

My husband, to this day, thinks it is hysterical to gently put me down in front of others. He is convinced that everyone gets his "harmless" jokes and believes that everyone is laughing right along with him. Perhaps he is correct some of the time, and the humor may be appropriate in front of friends and family but not in a situation when there are admissions officers meeting with you.

The problem is that making jokes is simply too risky when talking to an admissions professional. "My wife/husband is so 'neurotic'" are not words you want coming out of anyone's mouth at an interview that can determine your child's educational future. Disagreeing with your partner about your child is also unacceptable during the interview. Get your act together and if, for whatever reason, you can't agree on a particular point get yourself a good couple's therapist before attending any meetings with school officials.

Discuss your values and your child's strengths and weaknesses before the interview. Try to reach agreement on the educational philosophy you are seeking for your child. Even if you are not in total agreement with your spouse, leave the disagreements and discussions at home.

It is critical for a school to feel they are accepting a family that has a strong affinity for their school and who wants to whole-heartedly become a member of their community. A family that shows ambivalence about the school or disagreement will not be strategically positioning themselves to have the best chance of being accepted.

In summary, it is vital to come across as two people who have common goals and aspirations for their child, even though this may not always be the case. You want to be likeable, positive, and as ideal of a couple as you can be.

4) Feel confident as a family, but do not show a sense of entitlement.

It is great to have pride in your family. It is wonderful that you know they are special. It is fabulous to have a job you love. Think all these positive thoughts and communicate them in your interview. This is important, but it is just as important to remain humble, real, and polite. No matter how important and accomplished you both are, look at these meetings as you would a job interview for a job that you really want.

At one interview a woman was asked to tell the interviewer about her child. Her incredible response was:

"Well, I'm just not worried about my child. She is extremely bright and will get in everywhere we want

because any school will be lucky to have her."

While that might possibly be true, most schools will not feel "lucky" to have to contend with this parental attitude over the years that this parent will be involved in the school.

In New York City there are so many bright, wonderful children from a multitude of fantastic families. Many residents here have interesting and unique jobs. Trust us, the admission staff has seen and heard it all many, many times. It is much more impressive when families, with all their substantial attributes, lineage and accomplishments, are humble, real and genuine!

5) Ask thoughtful questions showing that you have read the school's materials and visited their website.

This is critical. Admissions staff are unimpressed and turned off when a family reveals their lack of knowledge about the school's history and philosophy during an interview. If you determine that the school is not a good fit, do not waste everyone's time. You must do your homework first and research everything about a school and then schedule an interview! Even if it's a safety school.

For example, it would be a major mistake to tell the interviewer at a co-ed school that you actually prefer a single-sex education for your child. Yet we have this happen over and over.

Most important, try to enjoy the process of learning about the variety of excellent education that independent New York City private schools offer. Remember, the interviewers simply want to get to know you and your wonderful family a bit more. You should speak with pride, not with what could possibly be perceived to be arrogance!

Turn Off Your Cell Phone – A Cautionary Tale

This is obvious, isn't it? No!

Remember to always turn off your cell phone before school interviews, tours, or informational sessions.

Here is how I managed to violate this rule.

I arrived early to an information night at a New York City private school and took a seat near the front of the large auditorium.

I was enjoying the presentations until, about 20 minutes in, it occurred to me that I had forgotten to turn off my phone. I was seated front and center where it was hard to get to my phone without drawing attention to myself. The phone was new and I was not familiar enough with it to turn it off without looking at it. I surreptitiously tried to get to it, but gave up after several unsuccessful discreet attempts, hoping that no one would call or text (loud buzzing sounds).

The remainder of the evening was very tense for me. No one called, but I can still recall my stress worrying that a phone call would interrupt one of the presenter's speeches and all eyes in the room would be on me.

14

Connections

Having connections to help you obtain an acceptance letter to a NYC private school can be extremely helpful to some applicant families while confusing to others. It is difficult to know what to do with these connections and how to use them as you proceed with the application process. There are two types of connections:

- ***those that can make a real difference between acceptance and waitlist or rejection, and***
- ***those that can't.***

If you have a real connection to a school: current families that attend, an alumna who is close to your family, or a person who is currently on the Board of the school in which you are applying, it is always a good idea to have these people write a letter on your behalf in support of your family's application. Make sure that these connections are well-liked by the school community and that their support, in no way means that they are expecting you to definitely attend the school if accepted. If the connection says to you,

"If I go to bat for you, you need to make sure the school is your top choice, and if accepted promise me you will attend."

then save their letter for later in the process, once you are sure that the school is indeed your top choice!

Problems with connections arise when an applicant puts too much faith into a connection that can put in a good word for a family but does not have any real pull in getting that family into a NYC private school. A second problem occurs when a connection has a lot of input into the decision making process, but the family they are pulling for, are just not the right fit for the school.

*A school **WILL NOT** accept a family - no matter how strong the connection - if they do not feel it is a good match between the school and child or family!*

There are also some connections that DO have the power to make a difference and have your family admitted to your school of choice. However, the most common type of connections are the ones that can put in a good word on your behalf, but have little power to actually get you admitted. Remember, a nice letter about your family from a connection is always helpful to an extent. But more importantly, is this school the "Right Fit," and will your family and child be successful in this school community?

What if you have connections to many schools?? How can you make that commitment to a school early in the process...how do you use multiple connections to multiple schools? Most schools will not give you a guarantee of admittance before the deadline. AND very few connections can give you a guarantee that if they "go to bat," for you it will mean an acceptance letter!

What if you have a strong connection to your second choice school and a fair connection to the top school of your choice and both want you to promise to go if you get accepted.

This gets really complicated and there are no easy answers.

In the ultra-competitive world of NYC private schools, a family would be fortunate to have strong connections to any of their top three coveted schools. If this is the case and the school is a great fit, please use your connections where they are the strongest. Inquire if the others won't mind still putting in in a good word for you even if it might not be your number one choice. Honesty is the best policy. It is important not to burn social bridges or make enemies with someone who is kind enough to do you a favor and put their name on the line for your family!

15

My Child Is a Sibling So He'll Get into Our Other Child's Current School, Right?

Unfortunately, this is not at all an accurate assumption! There was a time when siblings attended the same schools because schools and parents felt it was important to keep siblings together.

However, with the increasing number of children in families that can afford New York City private schools, coupled with the increased number of overall applicants to New York City private schools, a sibling applicant is no longer a shoe-in!

And parents are beginning to understand that what works in a school for one of their children may not work for his/her brother or sister.

Why Aren't All Schools Sibling Friendly? This Seems Terribly Unfair!

It may seem unfair to the families that are already members of the school community, but it is not unfair to families who are qualified and applying to an appropriate school for the first time. Wouldn't it be more equitable for them to have an equal opportunity to attend a particular school?

Some schools feel that it is unfair to fill most of their existing open spots with siblings of families who are already in the school. Consequently, they seek to add new families to their existing communities.

If a sibling does not appear to be a good fit for the school, admission will be denied or wait-listed. This may seem wrong, but it would also be wrong (and perhaps detrimental) to admit a child to a school based solely on his status as a sibling. You would not want your child to struggle in a school, academically and/or socially, simply for the convenience of having your children at one school. There are hundreds of great schools in New York! Every child is not a match for every school. Parents and schools must try to establish the best fit for each child, no matter how hard (and painful) the reality!

A very dear of ours had to face this situation:

My daughter eagerly prepares for school each morning, happy to see her friends and teachers. She is thriving in all the ways one would want for their child. We are now applying for our son, a completely different child. I'm not just speaking about gender differences. He has had difficulty adjusting to his pre-school, making friends, learning routines, sitting still, and investing in anything for long. My husband insists we apply to our daughter's school, but I know the fit is not right. I finally convinced my husband to meet with the Admissions Director prior to applying. Why put him and ourselves through that whole process? We were frank with the Director and she, in turn, was frank with us. She offered great suggestions for schools, which might be a good fit for our son. Most of us want our children at the same school—for all kinds of legitimate reasons. But we have to be honest with ourselves for our children's well-being. If the fit isn't right, there is just no good reason to pursue a spot.

And another friend had this situation:

We had two children at a school we loved. My husband graduated from this school. Of course we wanted our third child there. We pushed the influence of sibling/legacy in our application. After seeing our child, his ERB reports and school reports, the admissions office advised us that the school, though wonderful for his sibs, would be challenging for him in a way that would not be beneficial. We brought out all the 'artillery' to obtain an acceptance. We treaded on our toes, and it worked. We got him IN!

Three years later, we found ourselves looking for another school. They were right in their original assessment. Our son struggled socially and academically. Our evenings were a constant battle over homework and other issues. What a relief now to have our son in the right school, where his personality and learning differences are being addressed in a more appropriate way. And most importantly, he feels so much better about himself.

When Will I Find Out If My Other Child Has a Chance of Getting In?

Knowledge is power! Consider meeting with your school's admissions director in the spring before your application is due. You will want to ascertain if a sibling policy exists. You may be able to do this via the school's website. Many schools send a letter explaining their sibling policy in early spring. Some even host a meeting to respond to your questions in person.

139

Potential questions you may want to ask in this situation:

- If my other child seems like a good fit, is he/she likely to be admitted?
- Should I be applying to a wide variety of schools for my other child?
- Do you provide early notification for siblings?

Listen to the Director of Admissions. If he/she tells you to apply to other schools, take this advice seriously. Don't deceive yourself with thinking: "This doesn't mean me. This school loves our family. The Director likes us and probably can't actually legally put in words that our other child will get in—but we know she will do the right thing by us when the time comes. My son/daughter will definitely be accepted!"

This can lead to heartache and bruised egos. The admissions offices generally attempt to give each family a consistent message, no matter how loved a family may be!

Listen and act accordingly even if it is not what you want to hear!

What Exactly is *Early Notification*?

Some schools are so sibling friendly that they inform current families about admissions early in the process. Some schools pride themselves on keeping families together and creating a community of families in their schools. They notify sibling families well before the ISAAGNY (Independent Schools Admissions Association of Greater New York) date. This is called 'Early Notification.'

Schools that offer early notification will give you the choice of early notification or choosing to wait for the ISAAGNY notification date. If you choose early notification you are indicating that your current school is your top choice. You are implicitly stating that if offered a spot via this process of early notice, you will accept.

If you choose to decline early notification, you are letting the school of your currently enrolled child know that you are seriously looking at other schools for his/her sibling. You are taking a chance that the school will not look at you as a committed applicant.

It is a tough call, but you ultimately want to be honest and find the best school for each of your children. We suggest scheduling a meeting with the current Director of Admissions of your older child's on-going school to discuss your options.

It's Confusing!

Some families do not choose early notification because they are uncertain whether the current school is the right fit for the sibling. They want the opportunity to hear from other schools before making their decision. This is reasonable. But you must understand that your current school is under no obligation to admit the sibling. So even if there is a strong sibling policy, if you turn down the early notification, you are essentially turning down the offer of priority.

This is where it becomes tricky because other schools will probably assume you are applying to the school the sibling attends.

Will Other Schools Seriously Consider My Child If A Sibling Is Already In A School?

Absolutely! In today's competitive environment, schools realize that parents have to apply to a variety of schools to be assured admittance and the best fit among their options. The days of automatically sending your children to the same school in NYC are over.

Another delicate situation. Schools assume that you most likely will want your children at the same school even though they know that not all schools are the right fit for every child in a family. If you seriously want your sibling child at a different school, you will need to clearly and convincingly explain your rationale in your parent essay and interview.

The Bottom Line: Siblings must apply to many schools!

Learn these facts

- Does a sibling policy exist at your current school?
- Ask for early notification (if offered) if you believe the current school is a good fit for your sibling child.
- If you feel the current school is not a good fit, visit other schools and apply widely. ~Make the case for your application succinctly and clearly.

16

Phew, The 1st Phase Is Over…Now What?

Well, unfortunately, the waiting game begins. Wouldn't it be nice to be able to tour a bunch of schools, pick the one you like best, and happily hand over exorbitant amounts of money to attend the school of your choice? It would be so nice if the school of your dreams accepted your child immediately and gave you the contract.

We all dream, but we have to awake to the reality of how this process really works. We know that after all your intensive efforts are completed, you are in for some months of silent waiting. Still, you can be pro-active! After you have completed your last tour, take time to reflect on each school you have visited. Review your notes. By now you will have a "gut" feeling about the schools. That feeling, coupled with your careful notes, should guide you. Select your top three choices. Now it's time to write your "Love Letter."

A "Love Letter?" What's That?

Think about a letter you might have written to your high school sweetheart a long time ago—the one expressing exactly why you love him/her and why you belong together: a "Love Letter."

Write to the Director of Admissions expressing your love for their school and why you feel this school represents the perfect community for your child and family. This letter should be succinct and thoughtful. You are essentially telling three schools that this is

147

where you see your family and where you hope to be offered a spot. Make sure you spell the Director's name correctly, which can be found on the school's website. This is not a "First Choice Letter" which is a letter written to only one school stating that if accepted, your child will attend. We will go into this shortly.

Why Not Write A First Choice Letter To The One School I Really Want?

It used to work that way. You toured schools, chose the school you loved best, and wrote a "First Choice Letter" letting them know that if you are lucky enough to be offered a spot, you would take it. Because schools interview hundreds of families for very few spots, they want to be sure that if they send an acceptance letter, a family will actually take the offer. (See, you are not entirely powerless in this process)

The Problem

Too many families began writing "first choice letters" to many schools and were gaming the system! They were often granted acceptance to multiple schools. Of course the family accepted the offer at their real first choice school, leaving the others with significant numbers of unfilled spots. In a process that seems like the schools have all the power, this might not seem like a big deal. However, it was a big deal to schools that trusted the family's written word. Imagine a sweetheart and your unrequited love when you were told how much you were wanted and then…another partner was chosen and you were dumped!

ISAAGNY (Independent School Admission Association of Greater New York) eliminated first-choice letters and replaced them with the current system of "Love Letters" resulting in a more realistic indication on your part.

Should I Be Talking To My Nursery School Director Now?

Yes! It is up to you to keep the director informed of the schools in which you are most interested. It is up to the nursery school director to then relay that information to the schools. Hopefully, the schools will let the Director know in a timely fashion if they want you as well. The perfect scenario is the reciprocation of these mutual feelings so you know there is interest by the school in your child. If your director has little information to give you from the on-going schools, then proceed with your letters to your top three choices.

One of our clients was fortunate enough to receive multiple acceptances to her top choice schools. The Nursery School Director was able to communicate this good news to the family prior to the notification date (the day when ongoing and nursery schools mail their respective letters notifying the families of an acceptance, waitlist or a rejection).

Our client was given the benefit of time to really think about her choices and make the best decision for her family. In this situation, she didn't need to send "I Love You" letters (which are usually sent at the end of the process before hearing any news from the school) because she kept timely contact with her Nursery School Director.

Should I Call the Schools On My Own?

Feel free to call the schools to check if your child's folder is complete. This means that the schools have received everything they requested: application, essay, ERB, and the current teacher's report. Your child has completed the playgroup visit and you've had your interview and/or tour. Most schools send a postcard in January to let you know if anything is missing from the folder. But it is okay to call ... ONCE!

Do not call incessantly (that means more than once, assuming you got your answers in the first call) with questions about your family's status or to reiterate your love for the school!

The nursery school director should be the one communicating with the admissions office, not you. Call only with questions relating to the completion of your application or to relay important information that was not covered in your meeting. For example, one family called to relate that they were moving and would not have a mailing address for one month. They wanted to make sure the admissions staff had a correct number if they needed to reach them. Obviously, this is an important and relevant reason to call, but calling about the perfect piano recital your budding genius just had was not! (Yes, this is a proud moment, but many applicants have those moments. Imagine if the admission staff had to field all these "important" calls!)

What if I don't have a Nursery School Director?

There are families who "home school" their children until kindergarten. There are also children who are in a daycare program. There are a small number of nursery school directors who are just not connected with the ongoing schools. What are these families supposed to do?

Well, there is hope! You would need to independently communicate with the ongoing schools in these cases.

Here is how: Make one phone-call to check if your file is complete. At that time express your strong interest in the school and communicate the fact that you have no one to speak on your behalf. Follow up with a "love letter".

This would also be the time for you to discreetly use your connections. If you have a friend who is a parent at the school or a faculty member, they would be your best advocates. Your goal should be to come across as a committed, interested and dedicated parent who wants the best for your child and family.

So, write your love letters, speak with your directors, call to make sure the folders are complete if you feel you must, and then try to relax! Enroll in yoga classes, go on vacation, or get lost in a good book to help get through this difficult time. You are not alone in suffering through this phase. If you follow what you have learned here this adventure should end with a smile.

17

How **NOT** To Get Your Child into a School

HOVER! Are you a dreaded "helicopter parent," one who hovers around the school, asking a million questions, staying close to the nursery school director at all times, lacking basic people skills and unable to read simple body language and cues to "hover" somewhere else more appropriate, maybe at Starbucks?

Do you see yourself in the above description? If so, you must behave in the exact opposite manner when applying to an ongoing school and interacting with key school personnel! Yes, ask your questions. Yes, show enthusiasm and love for a school. But do not hover over a tour guide or Director of Admissions. Do not make a nuisance of yourself. There is a fine balance between showing genuine excitement and interest in a school and being irritating and annoying.

We will never forget one couple who "LOVVVVVEEED" a particular school. They wanted this school for their child "more than anything." What did this family do to ensure that they would NOT be accepted?

Mom interrupted the Director of Admissions during her talk with a group of parents to share a personal story, one she was certain would impress everyone. Then dad decided to dominate the Q&A with his sage comments and lengthy questions. The Director had to finally intervene by stating her desire to provide others an opportunity to ask questions. After the talk, this couple stayed in close proximity to the guide during the school tour, complimenting just about everything in such an over the top way that the guide felt they were not at all genuine. They monopolized the tour with their self-serving comments and questions and they professed their total love for the school. But in the process, they jeopardized their child's potential acceptance by their transparent inappropriate actions. This is an actual example. Pretty shocking, right?

Think about this: If the parents act this way during a tour, what will the admissions staff think about their potential future affiliation with the school community if they ever become a part of the community?

Yes, admissions decisions take into account the entire family. Teachers rely on the admissions staff to accept great kids and down-to-earth parents with common sense who will be supportive, enthusiastic, and…who do not hover!

Overbearing and difficult! It would be fair to use these adjectives for the parents we just described. Instead, please think of and visualize the following adjectives when interacting with the schools you are interested in: modest, polite, and genuine.

Rude? There is no better way to illicit a "thumbs down" from admissions decision makers. Your behavior and demeanor is taken into consideration by the entire staff, from the individual who receives your phone call to the staff person who schedules your visits.

It's important to know that admissions staff is usually limited to one or two office support people who input the data, make the appointments, prepare the mailings, etc. The small size of this staff contributes to a close camaraderie. Rudeness to one equals rudeness to all. If you are difficult or rude there is an excellent chance key decision makers will hear about it.

I'll Call the School's Office All the Time So My Family WON'T Be Forgotten!

No. No and no. We know you have a lot to say and want to express your love for the school and your sincere desire for your child to be accepted by the school. We know there are unanswered questions you have that pop up. We know it is important to talk through your concerns. But please…do not call incessantly!

A call with a legitimate question is fine, but countless phone calls to the admissions office highlights you in a very negative way.

Sending numerous letters or e-mails is another way to bring negative attention to your family.

Remember, schools are regularly seeing and are in contact with hundreds of children and families every year.

Please think carefully before you reach out to your schools of choice and their admissions personnel. Be sure that you stand out only for your positive qualities!

I Know 10 families at this school. I Will Tell All Of Them To Stop Into the Admissions Office For Me!

Contacts and connections can be helpful to relate your family's values to the school in a trusted manner. But be sure to use them strategically and carefully. It's great to know a family that currently attends the school you love. It's great to know alumni who attended the school. It's fine to ask someone to discreetly and tastefully put in a good word for you with the admissions director. But be sure these families you are counting on have a good reputation within the school.

These friends should not call or stop by the admissions office too frequently. This would be overkill and reflect negatively on you! It's okay to have one family stop in to briefly chat with the Director of Admissions. Then carefully select one or two other families to write on your behalf. It's even more helpful if they also know your child well and can refer to him/her authoritatively in the letter.

Many families have many connections. If you are fortunate enough to have connections at New York City's private schools, be sure to use them wisely!

Was My Interview Yesterday?

Oops! Did you forget? It happens to the best of us. Not a great way to start out your relationship, but not a guaranteed rejection. The bigger problem occurs if you don't call with an explanation (that rings of the truth). Admissions staff works very hard to schedule hundreds of applicant families for tours and interviews. When someone doesn't show, the courtesy of a believable explanation is a necessity.

Honesty is the best policy here. Be gracious and flexible with any tour or interview they can reschedule for you.

Lastly, lose any hints of a sense of entitlement. This is a guaranteed "no-no." Unable to get the exact convenient appointment you wanted? Deal with it. Remember, admissions staff note your every reaction. There are many more fabulous families and terrific children than there are spaces in these schools. A parent or family that appears to be high maintenance is not going to be looked upon favorably by a school's admissions office.

I Am Going To Show MY LOVE For My Favorite School By Putting Down Other Schools.

Big mistake! Be professional and speak respectfully about all schools to which you are applying. If you can't say something nice, do not say anything at all.

If you disparage another school during an interview, don't you think the interviewer would wonder if you also speak poorly about their school during other interviews? This is a no win situation. If there are schools that you do not like, or you believe wronged you in some way, confide in your spouse or close friends only. Don't develop a reputation as a complainer or a gossipmonger.

Obtaining an application to a school is an easy task. Getting a tour date you desire is easily doable. Getting your child accepted? Therein lies the challenge! Don't make a challenging task impossible by your negative behavior. Take time for self-reflection and always, treat others the way you would wish to be treated…a wise lesson our parents taught us and your parents probably also taught you.

This was by far the most hilarious experience out of the countless tours that my husband and I endured during our son's application process for Kindergarten.

We were part of a group tour (around 4 couples) led by a parent tour guide. Everything seemed to go smoothly for the first part but as we were walking through the classrooms, one of the parents started flailing her arms, rolling her eyes, grunting.

Everyone including the parent tour guide seemed to be taken by surprise by her rude gestures. Her husband tried to calm her down by speaking to her in a foreign language but she just seemed uncontrollable. She couldn't conceal her irritation about the absence of a foreign language in the Lower School.

It was evident that the tour guide was completely put-off by the exaggerated reaction. She definitely burned her bridges at this school.

It was so bad that my husband and I wondered if any of the other schools would find out about her from people talking about this incident.

18

Married To Your School?

One of the greatest challenges facing families today regarding school choice is when they realize that their school is not the right fit for their child, especially if they have been there many years! When these families have been fortunate enough to be a part of a terrific school community and their child has made friends, yet they are not successful academically it can be a real eye-opener all around.

This is a growing trend we are seeing more and more. Sometimes, even when parents are cognizant of looking at their family values and who their children are, it can be almost impossible to predict where a child entering kindergarten will be as they grow and mature. As the work in school becomes more challenging, less concrete and more conceptual this can present a challenge to many children. A school with a definite structure may not be the best fit for a more artistic child. In the same way, a school without structure would also not be the best fit for a child that thrives in that type of environment.

This is one of the primary reasons that we steer our clients who are applying to Kindergarten away from only K-12 schools. The ones who protest that they solely want to do this admissions process once, we understand, but that is not always realistic. It can become especially hard when there is a sibling or two involved that has been extremely successful in a certain school setting, while the other sibling is struggling. We find that some settings, while they worked in the early years, are just not the ones that are going to bring certain children to success!

The key pointer is to pay attention, not be in denial and switch your child's school after it's too late!

Once your child is struggling, their self-esteem has taken a hit, and they are frustrated it is time to take action! Children will get into a vicious circle of not doing well.... feeling bad about themselves...not doing well...feeling bad about themselves...etc!

It is especially important to realize this sooner rather than later when you have an older child in the school and you know what the younger one can expect. Here are some questions to ask when faced with the possibility that your child needs a different type of school:

- *Is this really going to be the right environment?*
- *Is this school just too academic and my child is more focused in the arts?*
- *Is this school too unstructured and my child needs clear cut rules and expectations?*

The worst and the most frustrating thing to do is to wait too long to make the move for your child. Children take their cues from their parents and if presented in a positive way, while difficult, the transition will be easier. Some children might feel a sense of relief as they know they are doing poorly or just not happy in their current school and will feel grateful that their parents are noticing this as well!

Based on our many years of education experience

on both sides while in admissions and working with private clients, the best piece of advice we have for parents is if you feel your child is struggling in their current school, then it's time for a talk with them!

Ask them questions:

- *What do you find challenging about school?*
- *What would make things feel better for you?*
- *What can you imagine that would make you feel really good about going to school each day?*

Make sure your child knows that every school is not for every child and that kids switch schools all the time!

Parents who are in different schools already are a great resource to garner information on different types of environments for your child. Educational Consultants are another great resource to help you figure out the best fit for your child and family. Bottom line is you need someone who can really talk to you about your child's struggles and explain what would be the right environment for them.

And, of course, ALWAYS reach out to your current school to get their understanding of your child and what they feel would be the best move. When all working together, this leads to a happy, confident kid and parents who are at ease!

19

Rejections and Wait Lists—
What to Do??

After the time consuming process of research-ing, visiting, and interviewing at many NYC private schools, nothing is more disappointing than receiving a rejection or wait list letter.

What should you do now? Well, there is good news and bad news…

The bad news is that if you were rejected from a school, there is little to be done to reverse this decision. The school has communicated to you, without specif-ically saying this, that their school and your family are not a match. It's hard not to take this personally, but you need to move quickly to review other options.

If your child was wait listed, know this: Wait lists are real; they do move!

The wait lists are reserved for children who could be successful in a particular school. The primary reason for placing applicants on wait lists is a limitation in the availability of openings. Simply put, all the wonderful applicants cannot be accommodated. Another reason might be the composition of the incoming class. For co-ed schools, directors must be cognizant of the number of boys and girls in each class and the range of ages. Schools also typically want a mix of verbal and quiet children.

If your child is placed on a wait list, there are things that you can try to do to turn this into an ac-ceptance:

- *Immediately notify the school that you wish to remain on their wait list and will accept a spot if one becomes*

171

available. (Only say this if it is true!)

- *Reach out to your connections to see if they can put in a good word for your family.*
- *Send an email to the admissions director. "While we were disappointed not to receive an acceptance letter, we are relieved to know that xxxxxxx may still be in consideration for a spot which we would surely take if offered."*
- *You can choose to add one or two lines reiterating why you feel the school is the right fit, but be succinct! Remember, you've already submitted your lengthier essays in the application.*
- *Adhere to the directions from admissions staff. If you're told to check back in two days, call them in two days! If you get the director's answering machine, leave a message saying that you checked in as requested.*
- *You can reiterate the same in a follow-up email.*
- *Do NOT call every day. You must find the delicate balance in sharing your strong interest without annoying the admissions staff. In such an anxiety producing time, you must do your best to remain calm and cool-headed. Stay hopeful. Things have a way of working themselves out!*

Remember, if your child does not secure a spot anywhere during this process, public school is always an option. This might also be a good time to call an educational consultant to also look at alternate Private Schools!

20

And In the End

"The principle goal of education is to create men who are capable of doing new things, not simply of repeating what other generations have done - men who are creative, inventive and discoverers."

– Jean Piaget

As we come to the end of this challenging, yet informative journey with you, we hope that you have learned a lot about schools, yourself, and most importantly, your children. The emotional roller coaster of disappointments, embarrassments, hopes dashed, and finally some resolution will soon be behind you. We applaud your patience, thoughtfulness, and good spirits.

Our own children are now settled into terrific on-going schools. We have breathed that huge sigh of relief that you'll soon be experiencing.

Jennifer still thinks about the process she went through with her children in her efforts to find the school where they would thrive. She cringes when she recalls her daughter's inability to let go of her leg prior to the playgroup visits. She will never forget her five-year-old son exiting the ERB tester's office yelling, "This was the worst test ever!"

She remembers falling in love with a certain school only to be told that they were no longer accepting applications. She recalls every embarrassment, the heartbreak of receiving a wait list placement, and finally, the overwhelming feeling of joy when her children were finally accepted to a school that felt like "home."

For Vimmi, her move from India to the United States was nothing compared to the culture shock and enormous learning curve she experienced while going through the nursery and on-going schools admissions process in her adopted city of New York (her husband is still recovering!) But she and her husband came to understand that education represents freedom of thinking, expression, and communication. To be able to actively apply this in one's day-to-day school life rather than following a rote, restricted educational approach has been a most refreshing change from the education they received in their native country.

You have navigated the first steps in your children's education. Have confidence that they will become caring and responsible children, teenagers, young adults, and finally, grown men and women who will appreciate the firm and loving foundation that you have provided.

Appendices

KWL CHART

What I Know, what I Want to Know, What I Learned

What I KNOW

_____

_____

_____

What I WANT to Know

_____

_____

_____

What I LEARNED

_____

_____

_____

KWL CHART

What I Know, what I Want to Know, What I Learned

What I KNOW

_____

_____

_____

What I WANT to Know

_____

_____

_____

What I LEARNED

_____

_____

_____

KWL CHART

What I Know, what I Want to Know, What I Learned

What I KNOW

_____

_____

_____

What I WANT to Know

_____

_____

_____

What I LEARNED

_____

_____

_____

KWL CHART

What I Know, what I Want to Know, What I Learned

What I KNOW

_____

_____

_____

What I WANT to Know

_____

_____

_____

What I LEARNED

_____

_____

_____

KWL CHART

What I Know, what I Want to Know, What I Learned

What I KNOW

_____

_____

_____

What I WANT to Know

_____

_____

_____

What I LEARNED

_____

_____

_____

KWL CHART

What I Know, what I Want to Know, What I Learned

What I KNOW

_____

_____

_____

What I WANT to Know

_____

_____

_____

What I LEARNED

_____

_____

_____

KWL CHART

What I Know, what I Want to Know, What I Learned

What I KNOW

_____

_____

_____

What I WANT to Know

_____

_____

_____

What I LEARNED

_____

_____

_____

CHECKLIST FOR PARENTS

Name of School	Director of Admissions	Phone number	E-mail address

Research online	Attend Spring Tours (if applicable)	Request Applications	Standardized Test	Financial Aid request form	Submit Application (make copy for your records)	Schedule Tour / Child / Parent Interview	Tour School	Child Int/Playgroup	Parent Interview (if applicable)	Request Nursery school records for ongoing schools

CHECKLIST FOR PARENTS

Name of School	Director of Admissions	Phone number	E-mail address

Research online	Attend Spring Tours (if applicable)	Request Applications	Standardized Test	Financial Aid request form	Submit Application (make copy for your records)	Schedule Tour / Child / Parent Interview	Tour School	Child Int/Playgroup	Parent Interview (if applicable)	Request Nursery school records for ongoing schools

Notes on Schools Visited

School Name

_____

Director of Admissions

_____

Impression of School

_____

_____

_____

Observations for Thank You Note

_____

_____

_____

Notes on Schools Visited

School Name

_____

Director of Admissions

_____

Impression of School

_____

_____

_____

Observations for Thank You Note

_____

_____

_____

Notes on Schools Visited

School Name

_____

Director of Admissions

_____

Impression of School

_____

_____

_____

Observations for Thank You Note

_____

_____

_____

Notes on Schools Visited

School Name

_____

Director of Admissions

_____

Impression of School

_____

_____

_____

Observations for Thank You Note

_____

_____

_____

Notes on Schools Visited

School Name

_____

Director of Admissions

_____

Impression of School

_____

_____

_____

Observations for Thank You Note

_____

_____

_____

Notes on Schools Visited

School Name

_____

Director of Admissions

_____

Impression of School

_____

_____

_____

Observations for Thank You Note

_____

_____

_____

Notes on Schools Visited

School Name

_____

Director of Admissions

_____

Impression of School

_____

_____

_____

Observations for Thank You Note

_____

_____

_____

Notes on Schools Visited

School Name

_____

Director of Admissions

_____

Impression of School

_____

_____

_____

Observations for Thank You Note

_____

_____

_____

Notes on Schools Visited

School Name

_____

Director of Admissions

_____

Impression of School

_____

_____

_____

Observations for Thank You Note

_____

_____

_____

Notes on Schools Visited

School Name

_____

Director of Admissions

_____

Impression of School

_____

_____

_____

Observations for Thank You Note

_____

_____

_____

Notes on Schools Visited

School Name

_____

Director of Admissions

_____

Impression of School

_____

_____

_____

Observations for Thank You Note

_____

_____

_____

Notes on Schools Visited

School Name

_____

Director of Admissions

_____

Impression of School

_____

_____

_____

Observations for Thank You Note

_____

_____

_____

Notes

Notes

72800907R00115

Made in the USA
Middletown, DE
08 May 2018